HEROTICA

Published by Spines
ISBN: 979-8-89569-338-4

HEROTICA

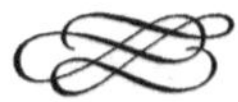

LAWRENCE 'LOVEALLWORDS' WHITE

CONTENTS

"ANTICIPATION"

They say good things come to those who wait

and that's why it felt like a year and a day

when I finally felt the suction of your Intake

it seemed as if I would have to really faint

after every deep breath that I would take

thoughts of you make me want to masturbate

while I put what I can eat of you on a plate

sop it all up; believe me it won't go to waste

even though they say nothing is better than the chase

but truthfully speaking the phrase is a disgrace

cause I love more than the chase, the tightness of your space *how you let me use it to wipe the whole of my face*

and it wasn't a tester, for I got more than just a taste

it was shocking how you even had sex with such grace

but you knew that just by the faces that I would make

that's why I kept an eye on everything I would anticipate

Now I'm waiting for the second time around, and the third,
fourth, fifth.

"2BANGHER"

PLAYING WITH THE THOUGHT VERY OPENLY

NEEDING TO TOUCH HER BODY VERY SLOWLY

SOFT IS HER TOUCH, WHAT MORE CAN I ASK FOR?

WANTING TO FUCK, ALL OVER THE BEDROOM
FLOOR

INTENSE IS THE AIR THAT I BREATHE FOR HER

WHEN I THINK OF THE TIMES THAT SHE WOULD
SHIVER

OVER AND OVER, AS SHE HUGS ME REAL TIGHT

WE CONTINUE OUR DANCE, AND SEE NO END IN
SIGHT

BUT THE FANTASY'S OVER, WE MUST BECOME ONE

I THINK, IT'S TIME **"2BANGHER"** UNTIL THE
MORNING SUN

SEX IS HER WEAPON, AND THAT RED DOT IS
ON ME

I CATCH HER IN THE SHOWER, CAUSE I'M SNEAKY

START PLAYING WITH THE NANA, TONGUE RING
ON THE EAR

BEND HER OVER REAL SLOW, SO I CAN HIT IT
FROM THE REAR

AND SHE LOOKS SO FREAKY, AS THE WATER
STILL RUNS

I HAD TO STOP FOR A WHILE, BECAUSE I DIDN'T
WANT TO CUM

SO, I GOT BACK IN IT, WHILE SHE PLAYED WITH
HER CLIT

THEN SHE TAKES ME OUT, SO SHE CAN SUCK MY
"_____"

AFTER SOME TIME OF PLEASURE, WE CONTINUED
OUR FUN

REMEMBER, IT'S TIME **"2BANGHER"** UNTIL THE
MORNING SUN

COCK-A-DOODLE DOO

"AGGRESSIVE"

Follow the roses on the floor, that room just for us

And we're not going to stop until I bust a nut

Girl, I hate to be rude, but I'm really horny

And I can see in your eyes that you want me

The shyness in you, wants you to hold back

But we both know you won't go out like that

You're going to take control, then fuck me to sleep

Forget the sheets, I'm not trying to be neat

When we fell on the floor we still didn't stop

The floor was bothering you, so you got on top

I got a splinter in my ass then I started to moan

You smiled because you thought it was your doing

We didn't even have foreplay, but I'm not mad

We only wanted to fuck, even in your ass

My bedpost was used as a cage for you

You're trying to get loose from the rope I tied you to

You asked me to pull your hair so you can scream

It was the type of sex you'd see on a movie screen

You can even smell the sex, just take a little sniff

Our blood was racing, that's why we were aggressive

LUST

"ANYWHERE"

With my ego it really doesn't matter where we at

We can do it a Yankee stadium with Jeter at bat

The place has no importance; it's the girl I'm with

Is she freaky enough, to let me lick on her clit?

People can watch that's no problem with me

We just must perform to best of our ability

The time in the park, up and down on the seesaw

I got a splinter in my ass from fucking so hard

The room full of people in someone's college dorm

Both of us released by the side entrance door

We could have got caught there but what the hell

We're both freaky adults, who are they going to tell

I remember the time at my job in the bathroom

My boss walked in while she was riding my bone

There was no stopping because we didn't give a shit

She even stopped riding so she could suck my dick

The time when I was on the peter pan bus

I first licked her clit, and then she sucked me off

The moral of the story, I don't care what I'm facing

It could be me and three women inside of a precinct

HORNY 10/25/00

"AFTER HOURS"

OPEN WIDE LOVE, BECAUSE I'M READY AND EAGER

EAGER TO HAVE YOU COMPLETELY SATISFIED

SO BELIEVE THAT'S TRUE AND THAT'S NO LIE

MY NAME IS NOT PINOCCHIO, OR WILL MY
NOSE GROW

BUT SOMETHING ELSE WILL, AND WHEN IT DOES
IT'S OVER

I'M AM NATURALLY EXCITED TO BE NEAR YOU

AND I COULD TELL BY MY PULSE RACING FASTER

BUT I'M SLOWLY THINKING WHAT I WANT TO DO

YOU LOOK SO PERFECT SPREAD OPEN FOR ME

BOTH SETS OF LIPS ARE CALLING FOR ATTENTION

AS I ABLIGE THEM BOTH, A IDEA SETS IN

MAYBE A LITTLE WHIP CREAM WILL BETTER
THE MOOD

EXCUSE ME, WHY ARE YOU SHAKING? IS IT TOO COLD?

NOW I'M GONNA LICK IT OFF NICE AND SLOW

CAUSE I HAVE A LOT OF SPOTS, AND NOTHING
BUT TIME

SO I WANT TO MAKE THE BEST OF THE SITUATION

I AM COMPETELY HAPPY BECAUSE OF YOU

WITH YOUR SOFT SKIN I CAN'T LET YOU GO

WITH YOUR GLOVE SO TIGHT, I DON'T WANNA LEAVE

WITH OUR ARMS AROUND EACH OTHER WE GO TO
SLEEP

GOODNIGHT

"BE QUIET"

I HAVE A NASTY THOUGHT I WANT TO SHARE
WITH YOU

GO DOWN ON ME, AND I'LL GO DOWN ON YOU TOO

THE PLEASURE IS MINE, THERE'S NO NEED TO ASK

AND WE'LL GO ALL NIGHT, BECAUSE I CAN'T
CUM FAST

WHICH IS GOOD FOR YOU, IF THE PUSSY IS TIGHT

IT'S TIME TO PLAY WITH WHAT'S BETWEEN YOUR
THIGHS

I'M WAITING TO MEET HER, SO WE CAN BE FRIENDS

AND YOU WANT ME TO RAM IT INSIDE YOUR
REAR END

YOU'RE NASTY ASS HELL, YOU ARE THE COMPLETE FREAK

I'M NOT JUDGING YOU GIRL, YOU'RE JUST LIKE ME

OUR MENTALITIES ARE TRULY ONE AND THE SAME

LET'S GO ONE ON ONE TO SEE WHO SCREAMS whose NAME

YOUR PUSSY IS WET, AND MY DICK IS ROCK HARD

JUST CALL ME CHARLES, BECAUSE I AM IN CHARGE

WE STARTED IN DOGGYSTYLE, TO RAM THAT ASS

AND I HIT YOU HARD THAT YOU STARTED TO PANT

YOU WANTED TO RIDE, CAUSE THE MOOD I WAS IN

I SAW IT IN YOUR FACE YOU COULDN'T TAKE THE INCHES

MY LOVE MUSCLE KEPT POUNDING YOUR SHIT

BUT WE HAD TO STOP BECAUSE YOU COULDN'T "BE QUIET"

SHHH

"BEHIND CLOSED DOORS"

SEXY THOUGHTS THAT SEEM TO FILL MY MIND

THE PICTURE I HAVE OF YOU IS FROM BEHIND

I ENTER YOU WHILE I'M ALL TENSE AND SHIT

YOU TAKE ME OUT, AND START SUCKING MY DICK

THE TALENT, YOU HAVE JUST MAKES ME CUM

NO SHAME IN YOUR GAME, YOU SWALLOWED MY NUT

*WHILE YOU'RE DRINKING, YOU START LOOKING
AT ME*

AFTER THE LAST DROP, I THEN EAT YOUR PUSSY

IT TASTE SO SWEET, SO I'M THERE FOR A WHILE

THE ORGASMS COME, HERE GOMES YOUR SMILE

I ENTER YOU AGAIN, CAUSE THE GAMES IS NOT OVER

FUCKING U HARD, AND GRABBING YOUR SHOULDERS

YOU SAID YOU CAN TAKE IT, SO PROVE IT TO ME

I DON'T WANT TO HEAR IT HURTS, OR STOP PAPI

WHO STARTED THIS GAME? YOU KNOW I'M A FREAK

NOW I GOT YOU BABBLING, AND CAN'T EVEN SPEAK

THE ROOM IS REAL DAMP, BODIES FULL OF SWEAT

IT'S LIKE A BASKETBALL GAME, NOTHING BUT NET

I'M SCORING ALL NIGHT, I JUST DROPPED FIFTY

*I'M **"MVP"** OF THE SEASON, BECAUSE **"I LOVE PUSSY"***

TRULY

"CREAMY LADY"

SEX MOTIONS AND LOTION ENHANCING
THE VIBE

EVERY TOUCH IS SO SOFT, IN BETWEEN HER
THIGHS

HER LEGS WRAPPED AROUND ME, AND RUBBING
MY BACK

TWO FINGERS USED TO SPREAD, AS MY TONGUE
LIGHTLY SLAPS

I SEE IT POINTING DIRECTLY AT ME, SO I SAY HI

INSTANTLY I SEE HER SHAKING, STARTING TO
MULTIPLY

SO, SHE'S SENSITIVE I SEE, AND I KINDA LIKE THAT

THEN I STOP SUCKING ON IT, AND BEGAN TO LIGHTLY TAP

BACK AND FORTH IN A VERY QUICK FASHION

THIS **"CREAMY LADY"** IS MINE FOR THE ASKING

ALL THE SENSATIONS SHE'S FEELING, IN THE TIP OF HER SPINE

IF I ASK, WHOSE IS IT? SHE WILL BE SAYING, It's **"MINE"**

SHE'S LUSCIOUS DOWN LOW, THAT I MUST SAY MYSELF

AND I KNEW REALLY QUICK, SHE TAKES CARE OF HERSELF

SO, I MADE IT MY HONOR TO MAKE HER SMILE

SHE WENT TO BRAZIL, SO I'M DIGGING HER STYLE

SO, I GRABBED HER LEGS, SO SHE COULDN'T GET AWAY

GOING FROM SIDE TO SIDE, IN A CRAZY SORT OF WAY

I ENTERED THIS LADY, AND SHE WAS FULL OF PASSION

TRULY THIS **"CREAMY LADY"**, WAS MINE FOR THE ASKING

TASTY!!!

"CAN'T WAIT"

In the anticipation of feeling your inner presence, I must say I CAN'T WAIT

As she walks away with a sexy face and such grace, her movements move me

Developing a fever around me because your lioness vibe has got me intrigued

Eyes mirrored for the bedroom look, which give a glair to call such a man in

To do such things as please every pore that has the pleasure of forming on you

Ready to breathe in the lustful scent that you release, got my mind racing

Proving the fact that I…CAN'T WAIT

The chest of treasure that follows the map that starts at your toes on up

Demonstrated in such a way non-verbally, that it makes you speak in tongues

Another language that you have not yet learn to speak, Damn I CAN'T WAIT

The liquefied moisture that oozes out of you because my lips have met yours

Making you feel like you are right back in that waterfall you chose to pose in

Tasting you so well that your pussy proceeds to kiss me back from the feeling

Squeezing that beautiful ass in the process because it deserves the attention

I enter her sanctum with aggression because that's what she wants and needs

Then the lioness comes out to ride, wiping her mane as she rides just the tip

Damn she got some skills, I bet she do with how tight this shit must feel

Too bad, she is in another state, but that won't stop me. Cause truthfully I…

"CAN'T WAIT"

"CUMSHOTS"

I'M GONNA TAKE YOU WITH ME ON A WILD RIDE

ON SOME THINGS I DID ON SOME CRAZY NIGHTS

LET'S TALK ABOUT THE TIMES WHEN YOUR AIM IS RIGHT

WHEN YOU HIT SOME SPOTS THAT MIGHT NOT BE LIKED

SHE SAYS OH MY GOD WHY DID YOU HIT ME THERE

I CAN'T BELIEVE YOU GOT THAT SHIT IN MY HAIR

I SAY I'M SORRY, BUT I CAN'T CONTROL THAT SHIT

BUT YOU KNOW I GOT EXCITED WHEN I TOUCHED YOUR CLIT

*DON'T BLAME ME FOR THE WAY YOU WERE
FUCKING ME*

NEXT TIME WE FUCK DON'T THROUGH YOUR B.E.S.T.

*THERE WAS THIS TIME IN A HOTEL WITH THE
LIGHTS DIM*

*THE FIRST SHOT CAME OUT AND HIT HER ON
HER CHIN*

THE SECOND ONE HIT HER RIGHT IN HER MOUTH

*CAUSE AFTER THE FIRST ONE, SHE JUST HAD TO
SHOUT*

I REMEMBER ONE TIME WHEN IT WAS TWO OF THEM

*I TOOK IT OUT OF ONE, AND LET LOOSE ON HER
FRIEND*

SHE GOT ALL MAD AND STARTED CURSING AND SHIT

SO, I SURPRISED HER WITH ONE RIGHT ON HER LIP

*SO, FOR ALL THE FEMALES WHO GOT HIT IN
THEIR FACE*

FROM THE BOTTOM OF MY HEART IT IS A MISTAKE

OOPS

"EXCITE ME"

QUENCH MY THIRST WITH SOME OF YOUR LOVE
JUICES

I'LL BE REAL GENTLE, I WON'T LEAVE ANY BRUISES

WITH SEX ON MY MIND AND YOU IN MY SIGHTS

THERE GOES A COMBINATION FOR A WONDERFUL
NIGHT

YOU WANTED TO START THINGS OFF WITH SOME
FOREPLAY

THEN YOU START LICKING ALL MY SPOTS IN THE
RIGHT WAY

THERE WASN'T A SPOT ON MY BODY YOU DIDN'T LICK

THE MOST TIME YOU SPENT WAS ON THE TIP OF
MY DICK

*NOW WITH EVERY STROKE YOU HAD TO BEGIN
TO GULP*

*YOU SWALLOWED EVERY DROP OF IT LIKE IT
WAS PULP*

THE SKILLS THAT YOU HAVE, GOT ME HARD AGAIN

*THAT'S WHEN YOU PUT ME IN YOU AND BEGAN
RIDING*

*I NOTICED YOUR SELFISHNESS WAS NOT TO BE
FOUND*

*ONE DAY, JUST FOR ME, AND IT SEEMS THE TIME
IS NOW*

IN THE 69 POSITION YOU HAD TO TASTE OH SO SWEET

*TWO THUMBS UP FOR HOW WELL YOU WENT DOWN
ON ME*

*SHE WAS FOCUSING ON ME; IT WOULD BE STUPID TO
COMPLAIN*

*THE GIRL WAS SO GOOD, I WAS CALLING OUT
HER NAME*

*EVERYTHING WAS DONE RIGHT, SO SHE WOULD
EXCITE ME*

*SO, TO YOU I SAY THANK YOU, YOURS TRULY MR.
HAPPY*

JOKER SMILE

"FREEKEY"

FREEKEY= A FREE KEY TO THE PUSSY

SEE ME, FEEL ME, TOUCH ME, TEASE ME

MAKE SURE MY BODY IS PLEASED PROPERLY

HOLD YOU, TOUCH YOU, NEED YOU, WANT YOU

LICK YOUR WHOLE BODY FROM HEAD TO TOE

WAITING FOR THE DAY TO SEE YOUR BIRTHDAY SUIT

HAVING THOUGHTS TO EAT YOU LIKE THE SWEETESS
FRUIT

YOUR BREASTS ARE SO SOFT, YOUR NIPPLES SO HARD

I WORK MY WAY DOWN TO SPLIT YOUR LEGS APART

*THEN I KISS IT WITH INTENTIONS OF MAKING YOU
SCREAM*

I FEEL SO CLOSE TO YOU LIKE I'M PART OF A TEAM

YOU OPENED YOURSELF UP, AND IT TASTE SO SWEET

I LOVE WHEN YOUR JUICES CUM ALL OVER MY MEAT

NOW IT'S TIME TO ENTER YOU, LET ME GO GET A HAT

*WE'RE GONNA START IN THE NORM, YOU ON
YOUR BACK*

BUT ONCE THE FREEKEYNESS STARTS TO SINK IN

I'M GONNA LEAN YOU OUT THE WINDOW

SO YOU CAN SCREAM AT THE WIND

*THE PURSUIT OF PUSSY GIRL TAKES A LOT OUT
OF YOU*

BUT KNOW WHEN I'M IN IT, I KNOW WHAT TO DO

THE MOST I EVER HAD WAS THREE GIRLS AT ONCE

*TWO ON TOP OF ME, AND THE OTHER SMOKING A
BLUNT*

GOOD TIMES 8-16-00

"GET DOWN ON IT"

FIRST THINGS FIRST DON'T BE SCARED OF IT

Its ONLY FLESH AND BLOOD WITH A HEAD ON THE TIP

THE INSIDE LIQUIDS CAN BE TWO DIFFERENT SHADES

WITH MILLIONS OF STORIES OF SEXUAL ESCAPADES

THE MUSCLE IS PULLED FROM BACK TO FORTH

*THE LUCKY ONES ARE ABLE TO BE HUNG LIKE A
HORSE*

BUT THE OBJECT HERE IS TO GET ME EROUSED

WE WILL BE PUMPING UNTIL SOMETHING SPITS OUT

*THE MORAL OF THE STORY IS, IT'S GOOD WHEN
IT'S OUT*

FOR ALL THE SHY GIRLS, PLEASE PUT IT IN YOUR
MOUTH

SWITCH

DON'T TAKE IT FOR GRANTED, IT MAY LOOK
HARMLESS

BUT IT SPITS OUT BABIES OF POUNDS AND OUNCES

THE MEAT ON THE SIDES FOR SOME DECERATION

IN MY EYES THERE IS NO BETTER CREATION

THE CLIT STICKS OUT TO SEE WHAT'S GOING ON

JUST TO MAKE SURE IF IT'S SHORT OR LONG

TO SEE IF YOUR ABLE TO GET WET LIKE THE FALLS

TESTING YOU TO SEE IF YOUR NAME SHE WILL CALL

IF FOR SOME REASON FELLAS SHE STILL HAS A FROWN

PLEASE MAKE IT YOUR DUTY TO GO...DOWNTOWN!!!!!

ORAL

"FANTASY"

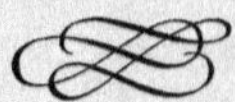

I HAVE MANY, BUT THERE'S ONE THAT STICKS OUT

BUT IT HAS TO BE DONE IN THE FEMALE HOUSE

THE CAMERA HAS TO BE SET, WITH ENOUGH TAPE

WITH A RED LIGHT DIMMED, AS SLOW JAMS PLAY

WE ALL WALK IN, BECAUSE I COULD NOT BE ALONE

SEE IT'S MORE THAN ONE, READY TO GET IT ON

THERE ARE THREE OF THEM, ALL DIFFERENT RACES

ALL PUSSY'S SHAVED, AND ALL PRETTY FACES

ONE SPANISH, ONE BLACK, AND THE OTHER INDIAN

WHEN THE CLOTHES COME OFF, THEY'LL START LICKING

THEY PLEASE EACH OTHER, WHILE I SIT AND WATCH

THE FREAK IN ME GOT ME PLAYING WITH MY CROTCH

ALL THREE ARE KINKY, AND THAT TURNS ME ON

NOW WITH LUST IN MY EYES I BEGIN TO MOAN

SO, THEY CHANGED DIRECTION, TO FOCUS ON ME

I HAD SIX SETS OF LIPS, THAT TASTES SO SWEET

MAYBE THE EXCITEMENT, IS WHAT GOT ME HARD

MY JUICES CAME OUT, THE FIRST ONE WENT FAR

THEY FOUGHT FOR MY CUM, A BEAUTIFUL SCENE

BUT THE BULLSHIT WAS, IT WAS ONLY A DREAM

OR WAS IT???

"GOOD MORNING"

THIS IS A DEDICATION TO THOSE WHO HAVE
SKILLS

AND THE ENDURANCE WITHOUT ANY EXTACY
PILLS

IN MY OWN EXPERIENCE, I'VE HAD A FEW BLOWS
MY MIND

BUT I'M TALKING ABOUT JUST ONE PERSON AT
THIS TIME

SHE MADE ME FEEL, LIKE SHE KNEW ME FOR
SO LONG

EVERYTIME THAT WE HAD SEX; NOTHING WENT
WRONG

WE WERE COMPATIBLE SEXUALLY, IN EVERY
SINGLE WAY

FROM BEGINING TO END, WE MOLDED JUST
LIKE CLAY

FROM THE KISSES THAT SHE WOULD GIVE ONLY
TO ME

BUT SHE AMAZED ME HOW SHE SATISFIED ME
ORALLY

TIL THIS DAY I HAVE MYSELF THINKING ABOUT
HER STYLE

SEX WAS A GIFT GIVEN TO HER, THAT DROVE
ME WILD

BUT UNFORTUNATELY FOR ME, WE COULD ONLY
HAVE SEX

ONE BIG SITUATION IN OUR LIVES, WAS TOTALLY
A MESS

BUT EVERYTIME I THINK ABOUT HER
CONTROLLING MY VEIN

THE PICTURE OF HER ON TOP OF ME, WILL
ALWAYS REMAIN

AND I REMEMBER ONE TIME WHEN SHE TESTED
HERSELF

TRYING TO PUT ME TO SLEEP, WITHOUT ANY KIND OF HELP

SHE WAS RIDING ME SO HARD, THAT I STARTED YAWNING

AND THE NEXT THING I SAID TO HER WAS, **"GOOD MORNING"**

GIDDY-UP!!!

"GUESS?"

SOMETIMES WHEN I'M ALL ALONE AT NIGHT

THE T.V. IS ON, AND THE CHANNEL IS ON SPICE

MY FINGERS START MOVING SLOWLY DOWN

SO THEY COULD MOVE AROUND AND AROUND

MY MIND IS FREAKY, IF YOU SEEN MY THOUGHTS

NOW's TIME TO SEE WHAT LOTION THAT I BOUGHT

I'M ALL BY MYSELF AND THAT'S REALLY BAD

I GUESS I'M GONNA HAVE TO USE MY HAND

SINCE THERE'S NO WOMAN TO PLEASE MY NEEDS

I'LL TRY TO DO IT MYSELF (OH! YES INDEED)

MY THUMB HAS THE POWER FROM THE START

THE OTHER FINGERS AND PALM, PLAYING THE PART

THE T.V. IS LOUD SO I CAN HEAR ALL THE MOANS

THE VEIN IS REALLY HARD, BECAUSE I'M IN CONTROL

I'M PLAYING WITH THE TIP FOR MORE SENSATION

SEE I'M A PRO OF THE ART OF MASTURBATION

NOW THE WEAKNESS IN MY LEGS WILL GROW

CAUSE THE TIME HAS COME TO LET OFF A LOAD

UHH! THERE THEY GO SHOOTING OUT MY DICK

TO BED I GO, BECAUSE I'M TIRED AFTER THAT SHIT

ZZZZZ 11/19/00

"BROWN SUGAR"

THE SWEET TASTE OF A WOMAN'S CORE

OPEN YOUR LEGS SO I CAN ENTER YOUR WALLS

THE PINK SHADE ON THE INSIDE, TURNS ME ON

*I'LL LICK ONE SIDE, THEN THE OTHER UNTIL
YOU MOAN*

THAT SWEET TASTE THAT IS LIKE NO OTHER

PLEASE DON'T BE SHY, WE DON'T NEED ANY COVERS

LET ME SEE EVERY INCH OF YOUR SEXY BODY

LOOK IN MY EYES AND SAY CUM INSIDE ME

BE THE FREAK, THAT I KNOW THAT YOU ARE

*HOW MANY POSITIONS YOU WANT, THAT'S THREE
SO FAR?*

BUT I KEEP COMING BACK TO THAT TASTY MIDDLE

CAN I DO YOU A FAVOR, AND LICK THAT CLIT A LITTLE

I'LL GRAB IT WITH MY LIPS, AND HOLD IT IN MY MOUTH

CAUSE I'M REALLY EAGER TO EAT A WOMAN OUT

NO MATTER THE TIME, IF SHE CLEANS IT'S ALRIGHT

I CAN TASTE YOUR SWEETNESS, ALL DAMN NIGHT

PLEASE GRAB MY HAIR, CAUSE THEN I KNOW YOU LIKE IT

AS SOON AS I'M FINISHED, PLEASE RIDE MY DICK

I NEED IT SHAVED, NOT HAIRY, NOW SHE'S A LOOKER

*I LOVE WHEN SHE LET'S ME TASTE HER **"BROWN SUGAR"***

SATISFIED

"HARD HATS"

WORN, TO PROTECT YOUR SOLDIER IN WAR

SO, YOU CAN FIND ANOTHER TUNNEL TO
EXPLORE

WITH AN EAGERNESS TO FIND ALL THE GOLD

TO MAKE THEM WISH THAT YOU HAD A CLONE

EVERYTIME THAT THEIR MINDS WOULD GO DRY

JUST GET THE GREEN LIGHT TO GO INSIDE

LOOK OVER EVERY CREVISE IN YOUR SEARCH

THEN THE COMPLIMENTS COMES IN SQUIRTS

OF THE LIQUID SUBSTANCE YOU LOVE TO SEE

AND THAT'S WHEN THEY'RE HAPPY AS CAN BE

CAUSE THE GOLD RUSH CANNOT BE STOPPED

WHEN YOU CLIMBED ALL AWAY TO THE TOP

FOR THE COALS, CAUSE THEY'RE GETTING HOT

LEAVE SOME OF YOUR PRINTS, X MARKS THE SPOT

SO, YOU USED YOUR TOOL, TO DRAIN THE HOLE

JUST TO SEE IF ANYTHING ELSE WILL UNFOLD

BUT UNTIL YOU'RE READY, KEEP ON DRILLING

THE RIGHT COAL, WILL SOON TURN TO A
DIAMOND

BUT FROM, Some Tunnel Decay'S, YOU WANNA LACK

PLEASE TRY TO REMEMBER TO WEAR **"HARD HATS"**

LATEX

"HEAD OR TAILS"

A LOT OF WOMEN HAVE THEIR OWN REASONS

BUT SOME SAY NO, FOR SOME OTHER MEANINGS

BUT I HAVE THE PERFECT GAME, IF YOU'RE A MAN

EVEN WHEN LITTLE RED, TRIES TO RUIN YOUR PLANS

JUST KEEP IN MIND, THAT YOUR GIRL WANTS IT TOO

AND CONVINCE HER, THAT'S SHE'S GOOD AT WHAT SHE DO

PLUS, EVERY PART OF HER BODY, HAS TURNED YOU ON

MYSTERIOUSLY (HINT! HINT!), ON COMES HER FAVORITE SONG

IF SHE SAID SHE HAD A HEADACHE, THAT LIE HAS FAILED

THEN ASKS HER 1 QUESTION, HOW YOU WANT IT?" **<u>HEAD OR TAILS</u>**"

"<u>HEAD</u>", IS THE TREATMENT, SHE GIVES TO YOUR POKER

"<u>TAILS</u>", IS THE HOLE, AS YOU WILL DADDY LONG STROKER

AND SHE GIVES YOU **"<u>HEAD</u>"**, LIKE SHE INVENTED THAT SHIT

AND YOU'RE WORKING ON HER **"<u>TAIL</u>"**, BUT YOU WON'T QUIT

ONE HOLE YOU CAN'T ENTER, BUT YOU PLEASE HER ANYWAY

CAUSE WHEN THE RED FLAG GOES, THE FAVOR YOU'LL REPAY

SO, SHE'LL PLAY **"<u>HEAD</u>"** OF THE CLASS, AND TAKE DICTATION

HALF OF A WOMAN, IS BETTER THAN DOING MASTERBATION

I'M LETTING OUT A SECRET, AND THIS PLAN WILL NOT FAIL

JUST THROW THE COIN IN THE AIR, AND CALL **<u>"HEAD OR TAILS"</u>**

BOTH

"HOME RUN"

STEPPING TO THE PLATE, READY FOR ANYTHING

BUT I KNOW WHAT WOULD MEAN EVERYTHING

THE CHANCE TO SWING FOR THE FENCES

AS SHE WEARS THOSE "ABLES" THAT YOU CAN'T MENTION

AS WE GO FOR THE **"HOME RUN"**

WE JUST RECENTLY GOT PASSED FIRST BASE

BOY, DO I LIKE THE LIPS ON HER FACE

AND I HIT A BASE HIT AT THE SAME TIME

IT WAS A PERFECT SHOT, RIGHT DOWN THE LINE

ON OUR WAY TO THAT **"HOME RUN"**

BUT NOW I FLY PASS SECOND WITHOUT STOPPING

ONLY BECAUSE I KNOW CLOHTES ARE DROPPING

AND SO ARE THE CALLS THAT ARE IN PLAY

BUT THE BAT HAS BEEN TOLD TO SWING AWAY

JUST FOR THE CHANCE OF A **"HOME RUN"**

SO NOW I JUST TOUCHED THE THIRD BASE BAG

SHE'S EATING A FRANK, THAT MADE HER GAG

SHE WAVES ME IN, TO THE BASE THAT I NEED

I JUST HOPE I DON'T MAKE ANY SUNFLOWER
SEEDS

DURING MY INSIDE THE PARK **"HOME RUN"**

DINGER!!!

"HORN DOG"

I CAN'T HELP IT, WOMEN ARE MY DEATH

ANY ONE I SEE, TAKE IT STEP BY STEP

WITH MY EYES, I CAN SEE THEM

AND THE HUNGER INSIDE IS A NORMAL TREND

FROM THE HEIGHT, THAT SHE MAY HAVE

OR MAYBE THE CUTENESS IN HER LAUGH

THAT CONTINUOUS SMILE ON HER FACE

THAT CAN LIGHT UP ANY SPACE

WITH ALL THE SUGAR AND SPICE

ADDS UP TO BE MORE THAT NICE

THAT'S WHY IT'S HARD TO CONTROL ME

TOO MANY WOMEN TO FULFILL A FANSTASY

A CREATION THAT WILL NEVER HAVE AN EQUAL

THAT'S WHY A LOT OF MEN ARE SEE THROUGH

THEY CAN TELL WHEN WE ARE ATTRACTED

THEY ARE THE FRIDGE, AND I'M THE MAGNET

TRYING TO GET TO STICK TO HER LIPS

MASSAGING HER BACK, AND SUCKING HER **"TITS"**

LOVING HER SLOWLY, ALL NIGHT LONG

YOU'RE THE REASON, WHY WE ARE **"HORN DOGS"**

TRUE!!

"HORNY TOAD"

SEX POSITIONS FILL MY MIND IN EVERY WAY

IT COULD BE **"69"** TIMES DURING THE DAY

I LOVE TO **"EAT"**, SO I ALWAYS CARRY A **"SPOON"**

SO, FOLLOW ME, FOR THE MEETING IN MY BEDROOM

THAT WILL HAVE, ONLY ONE MISSION IN MIND

I SEE NOTHING WRONG WITH A LITTLE BUMP N GRIND

CAUSE I'M SINGLE, WITH A FEW CHICKS ON THE SIDE

BUT I NEED A GIRL WHO CAN RIDE, RIDE, RIDE

SO I CAN TALK ABOUT HOW WELL SHE RODE

THE TOOL OF A MAN WHO IS A TRUE **<u>HORNY TOAD</u>**"

IN EVERY WAY, SHAPE, FORM AND FASHION

TELL YOU RIGHT NOW, I'M YOURS FOR THE ASKING

IF YOU'RE THE TYPE OF WOMAN, WHO TAKES BACKSHOTS

AND WHEN I LET LOOSE, YOU WILL SWALLOW EVERY DROP

THERE IS NO TIME FOR NO'S, AND ALL DOORS ARE CLOSED

WHILE I LICK ON THE THOSE LIPS NOT UNDER YOUR NOSE

FOR MY INTERESTS ARE PEEKED, AND MY SOLDIER IS TOO

NOW COULD IT BE TIME FOR ME TO FINALLY ENTER YOU?

CAUSE I THNK SO, CAUSE THAT IS THE PLAYA CODE

PLUS I'M DEFINED IN THE DICTIONARY AS A **<u>"HORNY TOAD"</u>**

WATCH THE TONGUE!!!

"I GOT SKILLZ"

ON A SCALE FROM ONE TO TEN I'M ABOUT A SIX

BUT BETS BELIEVE IN THE BEDROOM I'M THROWING
THE DICK

I DON'T WEAR A WATCH, SO THERE IS NO TIME TO
PLAY GAMES

YOU BETTER BELIEVE, IF WERE FUCKING, YOU'LL SAY
MY NAME

I'M GONNA MAKE YOU WANNA DO IT AGAIN AND
AGAIN

AND LICK SPOTS, YOU THOUGHT COULDN'T BE
REACHED BACK WHEN

WHEN YOU WAS WITH CATS THAT COULDN'T SEX YOU
RIGHT

NOW YOU ARE HERE, WITH ME, SPENDING THE NIGHT

*AND EVERYTHING FEELS TIGHT, YOU NEED A BITE, R
U ALRIGHT?*

*CAN I CALL YOU FOR ANOTHER ROUND IN THE
MIDDLE OF THE NIGHT?*

*SEE I LIKE TO SEE WOMEN PLEASED FROM
BEGINNING TO END*

*I AIN'T HERE TO MAKE FRIENDS, OH I NEED YOU
TO BEND*

OVER, SLOWER, WE GOT NOTHING BUT TIME

*YOU WANT YOUR BREASTS SUCKED; I'LL GO FROM
LEFT TO RIGHT*

*AND I'LL SUCK ON YOUR NIPPLE, AS IF IT WAS MY
FIRST BOTTLE*

*PLEASING THE SHIT OUT OF YOU IS MY FUCKING
MTTO*

OH, ANOTHER THING I DON'T CUM REAL QUICK

*I CAN GO FOR TWO HOUR STRETCHES, AND NOT LEFT
OFF YET*

CAUSE I'M A CAPRICORN SO I CAN RAM ALL DAY

*IF YOU BEEN WITH ONE, YOU UNDERSTAND THE
WORDS I SAY*

CAUSE OUR MENTALITIES ARE REAL, WE GO ALL OUT

*I'LL MAKE ANY WOMAN SMILE, AND THAT'S WITHOUT
A DOUBT*

67

FACTS

"I TOLD YOU"

MY ONLY PURPOSE IS TO COME AND PLEASE YOU

JUST BECAUSE YOU QUESTION THINGS I CAN DO

AND FOR WHATEVER REASON, YOU'RE BELIEVING THAT

STRICKLY SPECULATION, WITHOUT NO ADDED FACTS

I'M GONNA TURN YOU INTO MY SLAVE, WITH MY RHYTHM

YOU ASKED FOR MY ALL, AND THAT'S WHAT I'M GIVEN

SO, PREPARE YOURSELF, FOR THE CHALLENGE YOU TOOK

AND I WILL LOVE PLEASING YOU, YOU'RE OFF THE HOOK

GET THEM LEGS SHAKING, UNTIL YOU DON'T KNOW WHAT TO DO

AND ALL THAT I WILL SAY AT THE END IS, "<u>I TOLD YOU</u>"

SO WHY WOULD YOU TEST SOMEONE, YOU DON'T KNOW

ESPECIALLY A MAN LIKE ME, WHO HAS A VERY HUGE EGO

AND THAT MEANS I WON'T LET YOU GO, UNTIL YOU'RE PLEASED

MAKE YOU START TO LOVE ME, CAUSE YOU LIKE TO BE TEASED

ON EVERY PART OF YOUR BODY, FROM WHAT I CAN TELL

THAT'S WHY I WONDER IF YOU'RE THE TYPE THAT WILL YELL

MAKING ME MORE AGGRESSIVE, BECAUSE I LIKE TO HEAR MOANS

AND TO BE HONEST WITH YOU, CAN YOU RIDE ME CROME

CAUSE I THINK THAT YOU REALLY KNOW WHAT
TO DO

BUT YOUNG LADY WHEN WE'RE DONE, YOU'LL
HEAR **<u>I TOLD YOU</u>**

YOU'LL GET IT!!!

"I'M FIESTY"

I GET ALL IN IT, LICK IT AND SPLIT IT

WITH MY LIP, OR MY FINGER TIP

OR YOU MIGHT CATCH A SPIT, **<u>YOU NICE CLIT</u>**

DO YOU WANNA FEEL MY TONGUE?

REAL QUICK, WHILE YOU SUCK ON MY

___________?

OH SHIT!!! I HOPE YOU'RE READY FOR IT

<u>YOU NICE CLIT</u>, HOW THE HELL YOU DOING MISS?

WHERE YOU BEEN? SHIT! WE WERE SO FREQUENT

YOU'RE SO HEAVEN SENT, HOW I MISS THAT SCENT

AND THAT'S WHEN I FLIP, THEN LEGS I SPLIT

COME FEEL THE TONGUE WITH A PIERCING IN IT

ON MY FACE YOU'LL SIT, PLEASE DON'T SHIT

I'M SORRY, I HAD TO SAY THAT, TO MAKE YOU LAUGH A BIT

BUT NOW I'M BACK WITH MISS, REMEMBER **<u>YOU NICE CLIT</u>**"

SHE MOANS OUT LOUD, FINGERS ON HER TITS

THEN I SOME HOW I START TO GET FEVERISH

BLOOD STARTS RACING A BIT, I START SHAKING & SHIT

AND THAT ONLY MEANS, I'M REALLY FUCKING IN TO IT

I'M FLOWING SO QUICK, HER ORGAMS REACH DOUBLE DIGITS

OH SHIT!!! **<u>"YOU NICE CLIT"</u>**, WHY DON'T YOU REST A BIT

CAUSE **<u>"I'M FIESTY"</u>** WHEN MY LIPS TIP THE CLIT

TRUE!!!11/09/01 1:54 PM

"JUST BRING IT"

THIS IS FOR WOMEN WHO THINK THEY'RE ALL THAT

DON'T TALK SHIT, SHOW ME WHAT YOU'RE ABOUT

IF YOUR STUFF IS THAT GOOD, MAKE ME SAY IT

I DON'T HAVE TIME FOR LITTLE KID GAMES

MY MIND IS WAY TOO ADVANCED FOR ALL THAT

I WANT A WOMAN TO MAKE ME LAUGH

FROM HER PERSONALITY, NOT IGNORANCE

IT SEEMS THAT THE MEN HAVE TO DO IT ALL

FUCK THAT SHIT, LET'S GO HALF ON A BABY

IF YOU GET MY DRIFT

I DON'T WANT YOU IN FRONT OR BEHIND ME

I WANT TO WALK HAND TO HAND, SIDE BY SIDE

I'M NOT BETTER THAN YOU, NOR YOU ME

SO, LET'S SEE THE WORLD TOGETHER AS ONE

IF YOU PLEASE ME, I'M GONNA PLEASE MORE

AND THAT'S A PROMISE

DON'T TELL ME YOU SUCK DICK

THEN ALL YOU DO IS PUT YOUR MOUTH ON IT

WHAT THE FUCK IS WRONG WITH YOU? (CRAZY ASS)

I GET IT, YOU'RE GONNA ACT LIKE A VIRGIN AGAIN

COME ON ALREADY YOU KNOW YOU LIKE IT ON TOP

YOU'RE A CONTROL FREAK, DON'T ACT SHY NOW

THE DOORS ARE NOW CLOSED, "SUCK MY DICK"

AND I MEAN WELL, GIRL

OH! SHIT, THERE YOU GO, THAT'S WHAT I'M SAYING

SO DON'T TALK "JUST BRING IT" JABRONI

COURTESY OF THE "SMACKDOWN HOTEL"

ROOM 1127-20-00

"LET'S GET IT ON"

A GAME OF LOVE, IS IN THE MIST OF ACTION

SOOTHING AN URGE, THAT COMPLETES A
THOUGHT

AND A TENDER SPOT HAS NOW BEEN FOUND

FROM A LOT OF SEARCHING FROM A NOSEY SOUL

TRYING TO FIND EVERY SPOT THAT MOVES YOU

INTO A COMPOSURE THAT WILL HAVE YOU CALM

IN A SECLUSION OF THE ECTASCY OF LOVE

AS I PROBE EACH & EVERY ONE OF THE HOT SPOTS

THAT YOU FEEL SHOULD BE IMMEDIATELY
TOUCHED

DURING OUR ESCAPADE THAT WILL BE
FULFILLING

CAUSE WE COULDN'T LET GO OF ONE ANOTHER

FOR THE SMALLEST AMOUNT OF TIME AT ALL

CAUSE WE REMEMBERED ABOUT THE LAST TIME

AND HOW MUCH THE SITUATION WAS ON OUR
MINDS

DWELLING DEEPER WITH EVERY THOUGHT
PROCESSED

SO THAT'S WHY WE WOULD TRY TO TOP THE PAST

MAKING IT OUR DUTY TO GO THAT EXTRA MILE

TEMPTING US MORE WITH EACH STROKE OR RIDE

NOW WITH SEX IN THE AIR, AND ON THE BRAIN

<u>"LET'S GET IT ON"</u> WHENEVER WE FEEL IT'S RIGHT

TRUE!!!

"INTERCOURSE"

OOH!!! WHAT A FEELING

I THINK THE PLANS ARE IN MOTION

FOR RUBBING HER BODY WITH BABY LOTION

MASSAGE HER BODY TO CALM HER DOWN

TENSION FREE FOR THE FIRST FEW ROUNDS

THEN I START LICKING ON HER NIPPLES

MY FRIEND STARTS TO GROW A LITTLE

I BLOW ON HER NIPPLE TO SEE IF SHE'S SENSITIVE

AND SHE'S TURNING ME ON, BY BITING HER LIP

I START LICKING ON HER NECK, TO EXCITE
HER MORE

THAT'S ONLY A LITTLE BIT OF WHAT'S INSTORE

*I LOVE TO USE MY TONGUE; YOU'LL KNOW WHAT
I MEAN*

EVEN WHEN I FINISH MY PLATE, I LICK IT CLEAN

THEN I TRAVEL DOWN SOUTH, UNDER THE BORDER

AM I READY TO DO IT? WELL KINDA SORTA

*SO, I LICK THE CLIT, THEN GIVE IT A GENTLE
SQUEEZE*

I'M REALLY FUCKING HORNY AFTER SMOKING TREES

SOME OF MY SEX THOUGHTS SHOULD BE ON SCREEN

*CAUSE I LOVE TO HAVE SEX; IF YOU KNOW WHAT
I MEAN*

IF, I WAS ASKED TO DO IT AGAIN, I'LL SAY OF COURSE

THAT'S THE GAME I PLAY CALLED "INTERCOURSE"

ONE!!!02/15/2001 8:37 AM

"LIQUID"

Her eyes said it all, Come take what I need you to have, so I do without hesitation. Grab her forceful, and rip her clothes off, up against the wall she goes. She's moaning from the anticipation, so I don't let her wait Slide in from behind and lift her up, as I taste her nectar for the first time. The more aggressive I get, the more she can't take, screaming in a language that is not mine, orgasms can make you do that!!! Now she needs to suck, while her body still shakes, she tries, every inch of me, that developed into a great situation in her mouth. Her deep throat is amazing, now the other holes, because she is at the point where she needs to get FUCKED

Biting her bottom lip as she takes her saddle to ride

Saying my name slowly, L A W R E N C E, as she slowly takes that slide…

Her inner walls have a sanity that can make me go crazy...

She got me saying her name slowly... OVER AND OVER

I couldn't help but to fuck her until her eyes rolled back in her head

Her Juices were gushing out of her like a running faucet

The falls of Niagara didn't have anything on her tsunami.

The wetter she got, the harder I got.

Anticipating where I'm going to let off my cum shot

For all the places that I could have picked, she chose her mouth and swallowed my dick

Funny I didn't have a waterbed when we started...
DAMN!!!

Time Unknown...

"LOVE SPONGE"

ENTER THE WALLS OF LOVE THAT'S SOFT & SWEET

SO, YOU CAN SOAK IN THE WATER AFTER YOU EAT

AND IT'S ABLE TO ABSORB SUCH LARGE
QUANTITIES

X MARKS THE SPOT, SO JUST SPLIT HER KNEES

TO GO DIVING FOR THE TREASURE THAT
YOU NEED

PLUS, IT'S HELPFUL, IF YOU ARE FULL OF GREED

AND READY TO FEEL ALL THE WARMTH OF HER

IN HER SPOT THAT IS USUALLY SURRONDED
BY FUR

SO, IF YOUR FACUET IS COLD, AND YOU NEED A GLOVE

TAKE TIME OUT OF YOUR DAY, FOR HER **"LOVE SPONGE"**

LET HER SQUEEZE IT SO THAT YOU CAN FEEL AS ONE

NICE & SLOW LIKE USHER, IF YOU WANNA HAVE FUN

BRINGING LIGHT TO THE CAVE THAT ONCE WAS DARK

FEELING SO **"FREE"**, LIKE GIRLFRIEND ON 106 & PARK

SO, MAKE IT VERY CLEAR THAT YOU ENJOY YOURSELF

MASTERBATION IS GOOD, BUT RIGHT NOW IT WON'T HELP

HER SINK IS OCCUPIED BY HER FAVORITE SILVERWARE

AND NOBODY ELSE WILL EVER WASH THEIR DISHES THERE

THAT'S WHY MY BABY LIKES TO SHOWER WITH DOVE

HAVING ME ALWAYS WANTING HER SPONGE
OF LOVE

SEXY!!!

"LUCKY ME"

JUST FRIENDS IS HOW WE STARTED OUT

NOW I AM PLAYING WITH THINGS DOWN SOUTH

I LOVE YOUR NIPPLES, AND YOUR BREASTS ARE REAL

THAT ASS IS BIG, LET ME TAKE A FEEL

THE SENSATION, IS GROWING FAST AND STRONG

THE INCHES I HAVE ARE GROWING LONG

YOU GOT ME EXCITED, WITH THOSE THIGHS

THAT'S WHY YOU NOW SEE MY NATURE RISE

WILL YOU GIVE ME A CHANCE TO ENTER YOU?

OR DO YOU THINK I DON'T DESERVE YOU BOO?

*BE NICE TO A MAN WHO STANDS, I MEAN PAYS
ATTENTION*

FORGET ALL THE GAMES GIRL I HAVE AN ERECTION

SEE THE TIME IS NOW FOR US TO HAVE THAT DANCE

*IT'S CALLED THE BEDROOM BOP, TAKE OFF YOUR
PANTS*

*THE TIME THAT WE ARE WASTING, DOESN'T MAKE
SENSE*

*I WANNA FUCK YOU SO HARD, THAT I'LL MAKE YOU
FORGET*

*TURN YOU AROUND AND AROUND TO HIT
EVERY SPOT*

EVEN THOUGH IT'S COLD OUTSIDE THE ROOM IS HOT

*SO, I HAVE TO SAY, "LUCKY ME" FOR THE THINGS
WE DID*

MAYBE NEXT TIME YOU WILL SUCK MY DICK!!!!!!!!

BJ

"LUST"

AN UNCONTROLLABLE URGE THAT SOMEHOW
TAKES OVER

IT'S USUALLY AROUND WHEN YOU'RE TOUCHING
YOUR LOVER

A SEXUAL TURN-ON THAT DRIVES YOU CRAZY

ESPECIALLY WHEN SHE HAS ON SOMETHING LACEY

THAT SEE THROUGH TEDDY, JUST MAKES
THINGS MOVE

IF EVERYTHING GOES RIGHT, I MIGHT NEED
SOME LUB

SO, WE CAN MAKE THINGS EASIER TO SLIP RIGHT IN

I DON'T WANT TO HEAR THAT SHE IS HURTING

YOU CAN SEE ALL MY THOUGHTS, IN MY EYES

SO, EVERYTHING THAT WE DO, WON'T BE A SURPRISE

LUCKILY, SHE IS FEELING THE EXACT SAME WAY

AND SHE IS READY FOR THE GAMES THAT I WANNA PLAY

THE GAMES BEGIN WITH ALL THE CLOTHES ON

IN NO TIME, ALL THE CLOTHES WERE COMPLETELY GONE

SHE DOES ME, THEN I RETURN THE FAVOR

AND EVERY INCH OF ME IS WHAT I GAVE HER

AFTERWARDS WE HAD TO LAY DOWN AND RELAX

BECAUSE THIS SEX SESSION, WE TOOK TO THE MAX

AND FORGET SMOKING A CIGARETTE, WE SMOKED A BLUNT

CAUSE THAT'S WHAT WE NEEDED FROM ALL THAT **_"LUST"_**

COMPLETE

"MILKY WAY"

WHAT'S GOING ON BETWEEN YOU AND I

AN UNCONTROLLABLE URGE THAT WE DARE NOT TRY

THE LOOKS ALWAYS HAPPEN, NO MATTER THE DAY

*SOMETIMES WE HOLD BACK ON THINGS WE
WANNA SAY*

BUT THINGS DONE CHANGED IN THE RECENT TIMES

IT SEEMS WE'RE GONNA SAY WHAT'S ON OUR MINDS

AND I'M GLAD OF THAT, BETTER LATE THEN NEVER

PLUS, I LOVE THE TIME THAT WE SHARE TOGETHER

YOU KEEP ME LAUGHING, FROM THE WAY YOU ARE

*SINCE WE MET THAT DAY IN FRONT OF THE
SHARK BAR*

WE'VE GROWN TO BE GOOD FRIENDS, THANK YOU

IF YOU NEED ANYTHING I WILL BE THERE FOR YOU

*I TRY HARD TO RELAX, BECAUSE YOUR FRIENDSHIP
IS REAL*

BUT YOU JUST DON'T KNOW HOW YOU MAKE ME FEEL

THE SEXYNESS IN YOU, IS A REAL TURN ON FOR ME

*THERE'S NOT A SPOT I WOULDN'T LICK TO KEEP YOU
HAPPY*

*AND THE FUNNY THING, YOU PROBABLY FEEL
THE SAME*

*I HAVE THIS FUNNY FEELING, I'M GONNA SAY
YOUR NAME*

*OUR FRIENDSHIP COMES FIRST, BUT I WAIT FOR
THE DAY*

I LOOK IN YOUR EYES, WHILE YOU RIDE MY
<u>"MILKY WAY"</u>

SHOOTING STARS

"NASTY"

THE SEXUAL TENSION JUST FILLS THE ROOM

HER WHOLE BODY I AM READY TO CONSUME

BEWARE OF MY ACTIONS, BECAUSE OF MY THOUGHTS

CAUSE MENTALLY I'M TAKING YOUR PANTIES OFF

CARESSING YOUR BODY WITH THE OIL FOR MASSAGE

I CAN'T BELIEVE THAT I'M TOUCHING YOUR BOD

CALL ME A FREAK, CAUSE THAT'S WHAT I AM

BUT THE TRUTH IS, I'M JUST BEING A MAN

THE ESSENCE OF A BEAUTIFUL WOMAN MAKES ME THAT WAY

THEY CAN GIVE ME AN ERECTION WITHOUT NOTHING TO SAY

THE THOUGHT OF ME JUST LICKING HER NIPPLES

SENDS SHIVERS UP MY SPINE, AND MAKES MY BODY JIGGLE

TOUCHING HER LIPS, WHILE I LICK BETWEEN HER THIGHS

THE SOUNDS OF HER MOANS MADE ME WANNA BE INSIDE

WE GET INTO THE POSITION YOU KNOW SIX, FOUR + FIVE

AND FOR ALL THE CANCERS OUT THERE, SYMBOL 69

HER JUICES TASTE SO SWEET AND SHE IS DRAWING ME IN

CAUSE AT THE SAME TIME, WE BOTH STARTED CUMING

SHE KEPT ON GOING, AND GOT ME HARD AGAIN

THE FOREPLAY IS OVER, THE SEX NOW BEGINS

ROUND 2

"OF COURSE"

FOR THE NOSY PEOPLE OUT THERE, THIS IS
FOR YOU

IT'S JUST ME ANSWERING SOME QUESTIONS
YOU HAVE

FOR ALL THE QUESTIONS I LIST, LOOK AT THE
TITLE

FOR THERE LIES THE ANSWER YOU SEEK

THESE ARE JUST SOME OF THE STUPID QUESTIONS

IS EVERYONE READY TO RELEASE ALL THE
DOUBTS

PHASE ONE (THE START OF IT ALL)

1) DO YOU LIKE TO EAT PUSSY

2) DO YOU LIKE TO LICK ASS

3) DO YOU LIKE TO SUCK TOES (BUT ONLY SOME)

4) DO YOU LIKE TO FUCK GIRLS IN THEIR ASS

A GIRL ASK ME THE MOST STUPID QUESTIONS I EVER HEARD

5) DO YOU WANT ME TO SUCK YOUR DICK?

WHAT THE FUCK WAS ON HER MIND? (I DON'T KNOW)

6) DO YOU WANT ME TO SWALLOW IT?

AGAIN, WHAT THE FUCK WAS ON HER MIND?

7) DO YOU HAVE ANY HANDCUFFS?

8) DO YOU WANT ME TO PLAY WITH MYSELF?

9) ARE YOU A FREAK?

10) WHY DO YOU HAVE THAT TOUGUE PIERCING

FOR ALL WHO DON'T KNOW I'M JUST BEING ME

JUST LOOK IN MY EYES AND YOU WILL SEE...

"PERIOD" END OF STORY

IT'S WRITTEN ALL OVER MY FACE12:02 PM 07/22/2000

"PERFECT COMBINATION"

A controlled urge has my mind in a twist

Could my complete fantasy come to a rise?

Hopefully <u>something</u> will come to a rise

I have two beautiful women getting wet for me

And we all have been doing some thinking

I shouldn't keep my thoughts to myself

Cause I'm hard just thinking about what could happen

Two women, same sign, same height, both are freaks

One-man, different sign, same height, complete freak

With my thought said, they look at me and smile

Then they look at each other and the smiles get bigger

Uh oh! It's time to go to my house (now!!!)

When we get there, we experiment just a little

Then we eat, after that I start eating (hint! Hint!)

Temperature rising and your bodies yearning (for me)

Oh shit! The other girl finds her way in the mix

It happened before, but this one was special

We were playing chess, because I took both queens

Then they took each other for the first time

Relaxation sinks in, and everyone is happy

I can't wait for the next episode

Hay! Hay! Hay! Hay! "Smoke weed everyday"

BAR NONE08/11/2000 4:11:52 PM

"PIGS IN A BLANKET"

BOY, DO I LOVE THE TASTE OF THIS MEAT

LET ME GO GET MY FORK SO THAT I CAN EAT

THOUGH I WOULD USUALLY EAT WITH MY HANDS

JUST SO THAT I KNOW THAT I AM IN COMMAND

IT CAN BE SO APPETIZING, WHEN IN MY MOUTH

EVEN THOUGH I LOVE IT COVERED, I RATHER
IT OUT

THERE SO SOFT AND SUCKABLE, AND TENDER TO
TOUCH

I COULD DEFINITELY HAVE THEM COMING IN BY
THE BUNCH

THE MORE THE MERRIER, BECAUSE THEY ARE
SMALL IN SIZE

BUT IN THIS CASE, MY STOMACH IS BIGGER THAN
MY EYES

CAUSE I CAN'T THINK OF A BETTER APPETIZER
THAN THIS

THAT'S WHY BEFORE I START EATING, I GIVE THEM
A KISS

AND KISS IT UP TO GOD, JUST FOR CREATING THIS
TREAT

AND A WHOLE NEW DEFINITION FOR BEATING
MY MEAT

THERE USUALLY NICE AND WARM, WHEN READY
TO TASTE

AND IF I'M HUNGRY, I WILL EAT THEM ANY TIME
OR PLACE

PEOPLE WANT TO KNOW, WHY I WANT SWINE ON
MY FORK

CAUSE I'LL PREACH UP AND DOWN THAT I DON'T
EAT PORK

BUT I'LL HOLD THEM IN MY HAND, JUST SO I CAN
THANK IT

CAUSE ITS **Pussy I'm Gonna Suck**, THAT'S IN MY BLANKET

SIDE ORDER!!!

"ONLY IN MY DREAMS"

I WAS HAVING A TALK WITH THREE BEAUTIFUL
FEMALES

THEN ONE OF THEM HAD A STORY SHE HAD TO TELL

SHE SAID, DOES ANYONE HAVE ANY CHAP STICK?

THEY'RE NOTHING WRONG WITH YOUR LUSCIOUS
LIPS

I HAD TO AGREE BECAUSE THEY LOOKED NICE
AND SOFT

BUT A WOMAN SAID IT, AND IT TURNED ME ON

MY WHOLE MIND WENT BLANK, WITH WHAT SHE SAID

I SHOULD GET SMACKED WITH WHAT WENT IN
MY HEAD

ALL THREE ARE SEXY, I REALLY COULDN'T LOSE

TIME ALONE WITH THEM, WHICH ONE SHOULD I CHOOSE

I DIDN'T WANT TO, BECAUSE I WANTED THEM TO SHARE

HAVE THEM PLAYING LOVE GAMES AND PULLING HAIR

I CAN IMAGINE HER LIPS ON PLACES THAT I LIKE

EVERY PART OF THEIR BODIES ARE TEMPTING TO BITE

I STILL CAN'T BELIEVE IT, MY FANTASY HAS COME TRUE

THESE WOMAN CAN EAT PUSSY BETTER THAN I DO

AND I CAN EAT PUSSY, THEY ALL GOT TO SEE

AFTER THEY FINISHED WITH EACH OTHER, ALL EYES ON ME

I STAYED HARD ALL NIGHT, TO PROVE TO MYSELF

THAT MY DREAMS ARE BETTER THAN ANYONE ELSE

REALITY BITES

"PINK DREAMS"

FULFILL MY FANTASIES

AS I ENTER YOUR DOMAIN

WITH MY EYES CLOSING TIGHT

ONLY THE SHEEP WILL REMAIN

JUMPING OVER THE FENCE TO DRAW ME
DEEPER IN

THE SKIN OF HER LIPS THAT DON'T GRIN

BUT HER OTHER LIPS ARE SMILING

AS I ENTER THOSE TOO

WE SCREW, FINISH, THEN HEAD FOR ROUND TWO

AND AS WE START AGAIN, THE ALARM TUNES
TO WAKE

I HIT THE SNOOZE BUTTON, TO TAKE ANOTHER TASTE

FULLFILLING HER FANTASIES, AS I LICK HER INSIDE

SIDEWAYS IS THE MOTION AS SHE BEGINS TO RIDE

CAN YOU SLIDE ON MY PIPE ALL DAMN NIGHT?

WE FEEL AS ONE AS I MASSAGE HER WITHIN

THAT DAMN SNOOZE BUTTON IS ABOUT TO REACH TEN

AND SHE'S FLOWING WATER LIKE RIVERS & STREAMS

PLEASE DON'T AWAKE ME FROM MY **"PINK DREAMS"**

RESTING!!!

"PLEASURE"

TWO OF A KIND, CAME TOGETHER AS ONE

THE SEXUAL ESCAPADES COULD BE A LOT OF FUN

ME WANTING YOU AND YOU WANTING ME

LET US SHARE SOME REAL FREAKY FANTASIES

*YOU ARE TURNING ME ON WITH EVERYTHING
YOU DO*

I WOULD LOVE TO EAT THE SHIT OUT OF YOU

IT HURTS ME TO KNOW, THAT WE CAN'T TRY

CAN YOU IMAGINE YOU AND I IN THE"69"

I'LL LICK THAT CLIT, TIL IT CAN'T GROW NO MORE

I GOT YOU SO WET THAT SEEMS LIKE IT POURS

COME BLESS ME GIRL, WITH SOME OF YOUR SKILLS

GIRL SATISFYING YOU, I CAN AND I WILL

YOU MADE UP THE TEST, THAT I WISH I COULD TAKE

UNFORTUNATELY, WE HAVE SOMETHING IN OUR WAY

I WISH WE COULD BRING SMILES TO OUR FACES

WE'LL DO IT ANYTIME, AND IN AS MANY PLACES

AS WE CAN TELL THE CHEMISTRY IS THERE

IT'S NOTHING WE CAN HIDE, WE ARE VERY AWARE

SO, THESE WORDS I WRITE ARE JUST FOR YOU

I WOULD LOVE TO PLEASURE YOU AND YOUR
FRIEND TOO

THREESOME

"PLEASURE"

TWO OF A KIND, CAME TOGETHER AS ONE

THE SEXUAL ESCAPADES COULD BE A LOT OF FUN

ME WANTING YOU AND YOU WANTING ME

LET US SHARE SOME REAL FREAKY FANTASIES

YOU TURNING ME ON WITH EVERYTHING YOU DO

I WOULD LOVE TO EAT THE SHIT OUT OF YOU

IT HURTS ME TO KNOW, THAT WE CAN'T TRY

CAN YOU IMAGINE YOU AND I IN THE"69"

I'LL LICK THAT CLIT, TIL IT CAN'T GROW NO MORE

I GOT YOU SO WET THAT SEEMS LIKE IT POURS

COME BLESS ME GIRL WITH SOME OF YOUR SKILLS

GIRL SATISFYING YOU, I CAN AND I WILL

YOU MADE UP THE TEST, THAT I WISH I COULD TAKE

UNFORTUNATELY WE HAVE SOMETHING IN OUR WAY

I WISH WE COULD BRING SMILES TO OUR FACES

WE'LL DO IT ANYTIME AND IN MANY PLACES

AS WE CAN TELL THE CHEMISTRY IS THERE

IT'S NOTHING WE CAN HIDE, WE'RE VERY AWARE

SO THESE WORDS I WRITE ARE JUST FOR YOU

*I WOULD LOVE TO PLEASURE YOU AND YOUR
FRIEND TOO*

"PORNO"

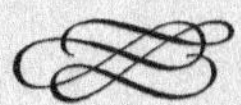

LET THE TAPE ROLE CAUSE I'M READY

READY TO PLEASE YOUR WHOLE BODY

TEMPTATION IS THE ONLY THING ON MY MIND

I GUESS WHAT I SEEK, I WILL SOON FIND

BEND OVER AND TAKE WHAT I WILL GIVE YOU

IT'S ELEVEN, AND WE WON'T FINISH UNTIL TWO

THE PRIZE YOU HAVE IS WHAT I'M AFTER

WHAT DO YOU WANT ME TO LICK, IT DON'T MATTER?

I'M HAVING ONE OF THOSE FREAKY THOUGHTS

TAKE IT ALL IN, UNTIL YOU START TO COUGH

PREPARE YOURSELF FOR MORE THAN SEX

I'M LICKING & STICKING, THEN GUESS WHAT'S NEXT?

IT'S THAT HONEY I BOUGHT, TO CHANGE THE MOOD

*YOU KNOW HOW SEX IS WHEN YOU START TO
ADD FOOD*

THE RED LIGHTS FLASHING, TIME TO LET ME IN

I LOVE THE WAY YOU FEEL WHEN I'M DEEP WITHIN

NO GAMES TO PLAY WHEN WE ARE BOTH READY

*LET'S DO IT DOGGYSTYLE, NOW CAN YOU HOLD IT
STEADY*

I LOVE THE WAY YOU TASTE, AND FEEL INSIDE

SO CAN WE END THE NIGHT WITH ONE GOOD RIDE

ACTION

"QUIET TIME"

A DAY IN THE LIFE OF…….

EXCUSE ME YOUNG LADY, DO YOU HAVE ANY I.D.?

YOU JUST DON'T SEEM TO BE OLD ENOUGH?

WHATEVER MAN, CAN I HAVE TWO DUTCHES

THE GAME STARTS HERE; I CHILL WITH MY PEOPLES AND I LOVE TO SMOKE. THOUGH I DON'T SEEM TO GET ANY SLEEP, BECAUSE I LIVE A LIFE THAT IS BLESSED TO BE A NATURAL HIGH.

FOR I WAKE UP THAT WAY SOMETIMES. I LOVE TO OPEN MY EYES AND SEE A BLUNT ROLLED.

WHAT A WAY TO START A DAY…….

I PROTECT THE MASTER WITH MY FINGERS AS MUCH AS I CAN. I FEEL IT COMING, CAN YOU SEE

IT. MY EYES ARE NOW CHINESE, AND YOU ALSO SEE A PERMANENT SMILE ON MY FACE. THIS IS WHAT I'VE BEEN WAITING FOR. I'M IN MY OWN LITTLE WORLD CALLED "QUIET TIME".

PLEASE DON'T SAY ANYTHING TO ME, BECAUSE I WILL NOT HEAR IT.

I LOVE THIS TIME TO MYSELF

CAUSE BEING ALONE HELPS ME THINK. I COULD THINK ABOUT MORE WEED, OR WHAT I'M GONNA WRITE NEXT. WHATEVER IT IS I JUST LOVE MY

"QUIET TIME"

"RIDE IT"

*THE EXPERIENCE OF SEX, COMES EVERY
NOW & THEN*

AND FOR ME I THINK IT IS BETTER WHEN

THE YOUNG LADY HAS THE SKILLS TO RIDE IT WELL

AND TO KEEP IT QUIET, NO TIME FOR KISS & TELL

*SHOW ME, THE CONFIDENCE THAT YOU HAVE IN
YOUR EYES*

CAUSE THAT IS SOMETHING THAT I REALLY LIKE

AND THAT IS SOMETHING THAT YOU'D WANNA DO

*CAUSE IT'S HARDER FOR US TO CUM, IF WE'RE
UNDER YOU*

PUT IT IN SLOWLY GIRL, SO YOU CAN TAKE CONTROL

IT MAY TAKE A LITTLE WHILE, TO GET INTO A ROLE

ONCE YOU GET IT, START TO USE SOME OF YOUR TRICKS

IF YOU CAN TAKE IT FULLY IN, LET HER SQUEEZE MY DICK

THAT WILL MAKE US BOTH HAPPY, IN JOCKEY STYLE

GO SIDE TO SIDE, THEN BACK & FORTH TO SEE MY SMILE

NOW TO REALLY GET FRICTION, TURN YOUR BACK TO ME

TREAT IT LIKE A STICK, AND TAKE FROM TWO TO THREE

SHE IS THE CLUTCH, SO LET HER CHANGE SHIFTS

AND IF YOU KEEP DOING THAT, THE VOLCANO WILL SPIT

*CAN YOU MAKE MY TOES SPREAD, SO I'LL SAY **<u>OH SHIT</u>**"*

*CAUSE THAT'S SOMETHING I LOOK FOR WHEN YOU **<u>"RIDE IT"</u>***

GIDDY UP

"SEDUCE ME"

WITH YOUR WORDS OR YOUR BODY

SEDUCE ME ALL NIGHT, CAUSE THAT'S MY HOBBY

DWELL INTO ME, WITH EVERY SEDUTION
YOU HAVE

YOU SHOULD COME ENERGIZED, CAUSE YES IT
WILL LAST

IT'S LIKE I INVENTED THAT DAMN WHITE PILL

THE ONE THAT TAKES OVER YOUR URGES AT WILL

JUST CALL ME **"X"**, CAUSE I'M A DUDE THAT **"RUFF
RYDES"**

WHEN THE PUNANY IS NEAR, I CAN'T WAIT TO
CUM INSIDE

WITH A **"FULL FORCE"**, SO LET'S MAKE THIS **"HOUSE PARTY"**

I'M A **"KID"** THAT LOVES TO **"PLAY"**, BETTER ASK SOMEBODY

NOW, IF YOU DON'T WANT TO **"DO ME"**, I WON'T BE MAD

I'LL STILL WANNA **"SEX YOU UP"**, LIKE **"COLOR ME BAD"**

BUT I SLIP INTO **"PINK"**, CAUSE THAT'S MY FAVORITE COLOR

AND I'M ACTING LIKE **"PRINCE"** YOU **"SEXY MOTHERFUCKA"**

AND IT FEELS GOOD IN YOU, AND THAT'S HOW I'LL TREAT IT

BUT IF IT'S THE MEAT YOU LIKE, BE LIKE M.J. AND **"BEAT IT"**

CAUSE **"YOUR BODY'S CALLING ME"**, JUST LIKE R. KELLY

AND I'M A **"NASTY BOY"**, SO PLEASE GET THE K-Y JELLY

SO, WE'LL MAKE SURE YOU WILL NOT LEAVE WITH A FROWN

A TRUE **"SWV"** FAN, YOU'LL **"RAIN"** WHEN I GO **"DOWNTOWN"**

FLOETRY

"SEXSION"

CALL ME THE SEX KING WITH A ROYAL CROWN

CALL ME A PUSSY CAUSE I LIKE TO GO DOWN

THE ART OF SEX IS LIKE A COMPLEX MASTERPIECE

IT WILL GO ON FOREVER, IT WILL NEVER CEASE

MEN WALK THE STREETS, WITH SEX ON THEIR MINDS

WOMEN DO THE SAME, AND ARE NOT FAR BEHIND

WE BOTH WANT THE SAME THING IN LIFE

A PARTNER WHO CAN FUCK THROUGH THE NIGHT

BE PLEASED, BECAUSE THE ORAL SEX IS GREAT

SOMETIMES YOU LIKE TO SEE THEM MASTERBATE

I CLAP MY HANDS TO TURN THE LIGHTS OFF

THEN WE START THE SEXSION, TO SEE WHO'S BOSS

SHE TAKES HER TIME, BECAUSE SOME WOMEN LIKE IT CALM

BUT I'M A FREAK, SPANKING HER ASS WITH MY PALM

WITH SEX ON THE BRAIN, AND THE SMELL IN THE AIR

IN THE SPOON POSITION, I START PULLING HER HAIR

THE PAIN HURTS, BUT SHE DOESN'T WANT TO STOP

THE EGO IN HER WANTS HER TO BE ON TOP

THE SEX WAS GREAT, AS IT IS ALL THE TIME

WE ENDED THE SEXSION WITH ME FROM BEHIND

THE STYLE OF DOGS

"SEX ED"

THEY TELL YOU ALL THEY CAN ABOUT IT

BUT TO ME THOSE DIAGRAMS ARE FULL OF SHIT

THEY HAVE PICTURES FOR ALL OF US TO SEE

BUT ON YOUR FIRST TIME, WAS YOU AS NERVOUS
AS ME

THOSE PICTURES ONLY HELP GUIDE THE WAY

BUT THEY DON'T SAY HOW YOU'LL FEEL THAT DAY

I WAS SCARED AS SHIT, AND I FIRED REAL QUICK

I LOST ALL MY STRENGTH WHEN IT ESCAPED
MY DICK

A YEAR WENT BY BEFORE I HAD SOME AGAIN

*MY FIRST AND MY SECOND, WERE TWO OF MY
FRIENDS*

*ON MY FIFTEEN BIRTHDAY IS WHEN I FIRST
GOT SOME*

*AND I LEARND WHAT I WAS DOING, SOME YEARS
TO COME*

FOREVER IN DEBT FOR THE INVENTOR OF SEX

IN THE SKILLS CATEGORY I FEEL I'M BLESSED

*IMAGINE, FREAK AND NYMPHO ALL ROLLED
INTO ONE*

AND I WON'T STOP TIL' I FEEL YOU'RE DONE

WOMEN BRING THE LUST COMPLETELY OUT OF ME

*THAT'S WHY I LOVE TO EAT, TOUCH AND ENTER THE
PUSSY*

*I LIKE TO PLAY WITH THE CLIT WITH THE TIP OF
MY HEAD*

THIS IS YOUR FIRST LESSON ON LAWRENCE'S "SEX ED"

CLASS IS IN SESSION

"SEX SLAVE"

AND I HAVE NO FREEDOM IN SIGHT

COMING ON TO HER, WITH ALL MY MIGHT

GIVING HER, STEVE MARTIN, YOU KNOW **<u>ALL OF ME</u>**"

JUST BECAUSE SHE LOOKS SO DAMN SEXY

AND THAT IS WHY I HAVE ALL THESE URGES

PLUS, THEY WILL HIT ME LIKE POWER SURGES

PLACE AN EXTRA POWER INSIDE MY BODY

AND IT'S ALL GOOD, CAUSE SHE'S HOTTIE

TEMPTING ME TO PLEASE HER BODY & MIND

AS I START TO SLIDE IN HER FROM BEHIND

MAKING HER QUIVER, AND RAISE GOOSE BUMPS

CAUSING ME TO SUCK ON HER CHEST LUMPS

BUT I DON'T STOP THERE, CAUSE I'M NO QUITTER

FOR I KNOW OTHER PLACES THAT I CAN LICK HER

LIKE THE BELLY BUTTON, BUT I'M NOT FRONTING

I GO A LITTLE FURTHER DOWN, FOR A LITTLE
SOMETHING

THAT TASTE SO SWEET, AND SURROUNDED
BY MEAT

EVERYDAY IS HALLOWEEN, PLEASE GIVE ME MY
TREAT

AND I'M NOT RUDE, SO THAT'S NOT ALL THAT
I GAVE

THAT'S WHY I WOULD PAY TO STAY HER **"<u>SEX
SLAVE</u>"**

WHIP ME!!!

"SEXUAL HIGH"

AN INTENSE ATTRACTION DRAWS ME NEAR TO YOU

BUT IT SEEMS MY THOUGHTS, ARE ALL I CAN DO

EVEN THOUGH TO ME, MISS SEXY IS VERY COMPLETE

FROM THE HAIR ON HER HEAD, TO HER PRETTY FEET

THAT'S WHY I WONDER HOW GOOD IT CAN BE

CLOSING MY EYES, PICTURING ME LICKING HER
PUSSY

SOFT & SUCCULENT, THE TENDER TOUCH OF MY
TONGUE

SHE IS THE HONEY, & I AM THE BEE THAT IS STUNG

HER RIGHT IN HER HIVE, WHICH DRIPS THE HONEY

MAKING MY DAY TURN FROM GRAY TO SUNNY

I WONDER IF BOTH SET OF LIPS ARE TASTY?

I'LL NEVER LET ALL MY THOUGHTS ESCAPE ME

CAUSE SHE WON'T APPRECIATE ALL IN MY HEAD

EATING SOME PUSSY, WHILE SHE PULLS ON MY DREADS

THEN I'LL SUCK ON HER BREASTS WITH EASE

WAITING FOR HER TO DROP TO HER KNEES

SO, SHE CAN PRAISE THE KINGDOM, WHEN I CUM

ON COURSE WITH MY DRIVER, FOR THE HOLE IN ONE

BUT I WANNA FORGET THE DREAMS, FOR A TRY

BECAUSE AT THIS POINT & TIME, IT'S A "SEXUAL HIGH"

RISING

"SLIPPERY WHEN WET"

AND THAT'S EXACTLY HOW I LIKE IT, ME, AND ALL
OF MY FRIENDS

I DON'T CARE IF I FALL, AS LONG AS I FALL
RIGHT IN

TO YOUR MOUTH, THE ONE THAT DOESN'T HAVE
A VOICE

IT'S THE ENTERING SECTION, THAT I LOVE TO BE
MOIST

SUCKING IN EVERYTHING RIGHT BEFORE SHE
WOULD RIDE

LET IT DRIP DOWN YOUR LEGS, SO WE CAN HAVE A
SLIP-N-SLIDE

NOTHING FEELS BETTER THAN THE WARMTH OF
A WOMANS GLOVE

JUST LIKE 50, I'M IN TO HAVING SEX I'M NOT IN TO
MAKING LUV

SHE IS GENTLE WITH HER GUMS, THAT SHE HAS IN
HER MOUTH

AND IF SHE'S WORTH THE RISK, I JUST MAY GO
DOWN SOUTH

AND IT WILL PROBABLY BE GEORGIA, SO I CAN EAT
HER PEACH

SHE'LL GO TO FLORIDA, SO SHE CAN GO DOWN TO
SOUTH BEACH

PURSUING HER TO TRY SURFING, SO SHE CAN
RIDE MY WAVE

IT'S THE THREE FINGER RULE THAT WILL PAVE
MY WAY

EXPERIENCING NIAGRA, AS IT WILL FALL
TOWARDS ME

THE WETTER IT GETS, THE MORE DAMAGED YOUR
BOARDS BE

AND I'M TALKING ABOUT THE HEADBORARD YOU
GOT ON A FRAME

I WANT YOUR PUSSY MAKING NOISE, FUCK CALLING MY NAME

ONLY THING I WANT YOU CALLING, IS ME ON THE PHONE

SO, I CAN LIQUIFY YOUR PUSSY, WHEN YOU'RE HOME ALONE

JUST GIVE ME THAT CHANCE, BECAUSE YOU'LL BE BEGGING PLEASE

AS SOON AS YOU GET THE CHANCE, TO **"GET ON YOUR KNEES"**

IT'S TIME

"SLOW MOTION"

LUSCIOUS TO THE TOUCH, I CARESS HER SLOWLY

EVERY INCH OF HER BODY, I WILL TREAT HOLY

FOR THE MOOD WILL MATCH THE EVENING SKY

AND MY EAGERNESS FOR HER, STARTS TO
MULTIPLY

SENDING A FIRE RACING UP & DOWN MY SPINE

SO, I CARESS HER WHILE SHE DRINKS A GLASS
OF WINE

GENTLY STROKING HER, WHERE SHE NEEDS IT
THE MOST

SHE'S ADDICTED TO OUR LOVE, AND SHE NEEDS
A DOSE

INJECTED, IS MY VEIN, INTO HER SOFT LOVE
SPONGE

IT'S ALL ORDER IN HER COURT, AND SHE'S THE
JUDGE

GIVING ME A SENTENCE OF 1 TO 3, WITH NO
PROBATION

WITHIN THE THIRD HOUR, IT WAS TIME FOR
EJACULATION

CAUSE I WAS SOAKED RIGHT INTO HER WAITING
WATERFALL

SENDING MY EMOTIONS RACING FROM ALL HER
HORNY CALLS

IT WAS LIKE WE WERE TRULY AT ONE, FOR OUR
ESCAPADE

SHARING MUCH MORE, THAN WHAT THEY CALL
GETTING LAID

THAT'S WHY IF FELT SO GOOD TO ENTER HER
LOVE ZONE

AND I COULDN'T TAKE NO MORE OF HER
CONTINUOUS MOANS

AFTERWARDS I MASSAGED HER WHOLE BODY
WITH LOTION

ENDING A NIGHT FULL OF LOVE, THAT WAS IN "SLOW MOTION"

WET SPOT

"SOMETIMES"

I WANNA WAKE UP WITH SOMEONE IN MY ARMS

I WANNA WAKE UP ALL ALONE

I WANNA BE QUIET FOR NO ONE TO HEAR

I WANT HER TO SCREAM AND MOAN

I WANT TOYS TO KINDA CHANGE THE MOOD

I WANT TO EXPERIMENT SO BRING IN SOME FOOD

I WANNA SEE IT, SO THE CAMERA WILL GO ON

I WANT HER NAKED, OTHER TIMES SHE HAS ON A
THONG

I LICK THE PUSSY AS CALM AS I CAN BE

I EAT IT LIKE IT WAS MACARONI AND CHEESE

I LIKE FOREPLAY TO TEASE YOU JUST A BIT

I HAVE A TARGET, AND IT'S DIRECTED AT THE CLIT

I LIKE IT NAKED, SO CLOTHES WON'T GET NO STAINS

*I WANT RIGHT ON HER FACE, SO I CAN SEE THE
REMAINS*

I WANT THE FEMALE TO HAVE ALL THE CONTROL

I WANT HER TIED UP, WHEN ENTERING HER HOLE

I THINK IF I WAS BORN TO ALWAYS BE A FREAK

I THINK THE FREAKY PART IS WHAT COMPLETES ME

*I THINK OF MARRIAGE WHENEVER SHE COMES
AROUND*

*IS JUST THOSE TIMES WHEN MY HIGH IS
COMING DOWN*

JUST MY THOUGHTS

"STRIPTEASE"

SLOWLY SHE WALKS IN THE ROOM

DRAPED ON HER BODY WAS A COSTUME

THE LOOK IN HER EYES WAS VERY RARE

SHE EVEN HAD SOME GLITTER IN HER HAIR

WITH THAT CLAPPER THING, TO TURN THINGS OFF

BUT THE LIGHT WENT RED, AND THE MUSIC
WAS SOFT

SHE TOLD ME TO HAVE A SEAT AND CHILL

CAUSE SHE IS GONNA DO AS SHE WILL

THE PERFECT SONG WAS PLAYING ON THE RADIO

EVER HEARD THAT SONG BY PRINCE CALLED
"INSAITABLE"

I'M WONDERING WHAT'S GOING TO HAPPEN NEXT

THEN I SEE HER SLOWLY START TO UNDRESS

A NICE DANCE SHE DID, TO GO WITH THE MUSIC

WHAT GAVE HER THE CRAZY IDEA TO STRIP?

THE SILK ROBE SLOWLY FELL TO THE FLOOR

"INSAITABLE" WENT OFF, THEN ON CAME "ADORE"

HER PLAN WAS BEAUTIFUL, RIGHT FROM THE START

*CAUSE SHE LAID ON THE BED, TO SPREAD THEM
APART*

*I KNEW WHAT SHE WANTED, WHEN SHE LOOKED
AT ME*

SO, I LICKED UP HER LEG, AND ATE HER SLOWLY

SCANDALOUS

"SWEET MEMORIES"

THE SWEETEST THING THAT I'VE EVER KNOWN

WILL STAY IN MY MIND, FOR HOWEVER LONG

OR SHOULD I SAY SWEETEST TYPE OF TASTE

FROM THE LIPS THAT DON'T HAVE NO FACE

AND THEY WERE ON, AND EVEN SWEETER PERSON

THAT'S WHY ON HER, I REALLY LIKED REHEARSING

EVEN THOUGH I ALREADY KNEW ALL MY LINES

EVERYTHING ABOUT THIS LADY WOULD SUIT
ME FINE

CAUSE I JUST COULDN'T GET OVER, THE TASTE
OF HER

IF I COULD PUT IT IN ONE WORD, I'LL SAY
"<u>SPECTACULAR</u>"

CAUSE ANYTIME I WOULD HAVE THE CHANCE TO
TASTE

I NEVER REALLY WANTED TO TAKE AWAY MY FACE

FOR SHE ALWAYS HAD A TASTE & SMELL OF FRUIT

PLUS EVERY NOISE SHE WOULD MAKE, WAS CUTE

AND I MEAN THIS FROM THE BOTTOM OF MY
HEART

THAT'S WHY I WON'T FORGET WHEN HER LEGS
WOULD PART

CAUSE THEN I WOULD MAKE HER FEEL RIGHT
AT HOME

MOMENTS BEFORE & AFTER, SHE RODE MY
THRONE'

SO THIS IS MY DEDICATION, TO MY SWEETEST
THING

THE **"<u>Sweet Memories</u>"**, SHINING JUST LIKE BLING,
BLING

I'M FULL!!!

"TAKING IT"

OF WHAT YOU ASK? THE GOOD STUFF

AND THE GOOD STUFF IS THE MOISTURE YOU
SECURE

IN BETWEEN THE THIGHS THAT YOU WEAR
SO WELL

YOU WONDERED IF I COULD TELL, I WAS GETTING
A DEAL?

CAUSE SUCH A GOOD DEAL WAS COMING MY WAY

THAT'S WHY I COULDN'T PASS THE TIME AWAY

EXCUSE ME MISS, DO YOU HEAR WHAT I HAVE
TO SAY

NOW WITH YOU, CAN I PLAY? TELL ME YOU
SAID O.K.

AND LET ALL THE BAD THOUGHTS GO AMSCRAY

SO THAT OUR SEX LIFE WILL BE HERE TO STAY

AND WITHOUT THOUGHT SHE PREPARES HERSELF

FOR A NIGHT OF PLEASURE LIKE NO ONE ELSE

COMING TO ME WITH BAD INTENTIONS IN MIND

WHAT LUCK FOR ME TO HAVE ON THIS LOVELY NIGHT

SO SHE TAKES FULL CONTROL OF THE SITUATION

BY STARTING OFF WITH FULL FLEDGED MATURBATION

CUMING AT SUCH A RATE, THAT IT EVEN SCARED ME

SHE WAS SCREAMING SO LOUD, THE GIRL HAD TO PEE

BUT ONCE I PUT IT IN, IT WAS MY WAY, I WAS MAKING IT

BUT NO SHOCK OF HER SKILLS, CAUSE SHE WAS **"<u>TAKING IT</u>"**

BIG GIRLS DON'T CRY

"TASTEFUL"

Succulent drips of envy liquefy down your thigh

From the thought of the pleasure, they amplify

And it then drips down to your knees, begging please

To once again have the chance to feel lips like these

Calling for another meeting is I, with anticipation

The size of her lips, has me wondering what I'm facing

I simply love the pussy cat when I am not the one chasing

Pacing back and forth wondering if I going to see it again

For I didn't finish my food at my lasting sitting

And with the time fitting, I'm finger licking

The monie in the middle let my tongue move a little

As I grazed the tip of your clit, with my bottom lip

And massaging with my hands the fat of your lips

I love how your pussy lips kiss, you sexy bitch

Cause I really want a face full because you are very tasteful

Extremely!!!

"TEASE ME"

A SEXY WOMAN WALKS THROUH MY DOOR WHINING

TALKING ABOUT SHE NEEDS TO BE ON SOMEONE
RIDING

SO, I SLOWLY GET UP, BUT NOT ON MY FEET

I SAY I'M HARD AS A ROCK, COME RIDE ON ME

SHE STARTS WALKING TOWARDS ME, LICKING
HER LIPS

PUT HER HAND ON MY LEG, TO START RUBBING
MY DICK

WHEN SHE WENT TO GRAB IT, SHE SUDDENLY STOPS

SHE PULLED SOME HANDCUFFS OUT, LIKE SHE WAS
THE COPS

I GOT A LITTLE NERVOUS, BUT IT TURNED ME ON

I WAS READY TO SEE WHAT WAS UNDER THAT THONG

*WHEN I WENT TO TOUCH HER, SHE SAID I HAD
TO WAIT*

THEN SHE PULLED OFF THE THONG, TO MASTERBATE

EVERY FINGER WENT INTO THAT MEATY VAGINA

I HAD TO ASK HER CAN I CUM INSIDE HER

THE ANSWER WAS NO, I'LL JUST HAVE TO CHILL

I'LL JUST HAVE TO DO IT, I CAN AND I WILL

*I GOT HARDER BECAUSE OF THE DANCE THAT
WAS DONE*

I KNEW THAT THIS NIGHT WOULD BE SO MUCH FUN

SHE DID EVERYTHING IN HER POWER, TO PLEASE ME

BUT IT WAS A GOOD IDEA FOR HER, TO "TEASE ME"

SEDUCTION

"TELAPATHIC CONVERSATION"

Within this vibe, the words are seen but are never heard

May seem absurd to the ones who try not to observe

Pay attention to those who you have become family with

A verse can be understood without a peep, it's a gift

Once you get the look or glance that you only get to see

Or find a love that you know you're synced completely

And the time that you've added together brings a bond

Having a sixth sense in the art of magic without a wand

It's a knowing of the other person or persons that comply

The unwritten word that's formed in the language of sign

But no hand gestures are used across to get a point

The party in our heads and we are having fun in this joint

Sick thoughts could be occupying what was a calm head

There is no vampire part assuming you could have bled

Hate when you're in biology class and the volcano erupts

No need to talk, since the period is here, we can't fuck.

BAD TIMING

"THE FREAK IN ME"

Sex dreams, sex thoughts, often fill my day

your pussy getS wet off the things THAT I say

help me pull your pants down, so we can begin

TONIGHT, the plans are to be more than friends

happy go lucky, the lucky get to be happy

I'm standing at attention, cause YOU'RE so tasty

SO, say I'm crazy for me being this way

if I had the CHANCE, I would fuck all day

tell me you like it, then moan in my ear

what you ARE DOING later, my plans are clear

see I love a woman's SMELL; it turns me on

let's both keep it up until the early morn

you want breakfast in bed, in the morning time?

just let me finish eating all that putang pie

I'm not finished just yet there is more to come

you need to wait until I bust my first nut

if you give me 100%, I promise to give you 150

can we switch positions to my favorite "doggy"?

there is sex in the air, and the bed is all wet

I wanna give you a night you'll never forget

NAT KING COLE 10/17/00

"XTASCY"

WITH THE BEDROOM PLEASURE, YOU'RE NOW MY SEX
SLAVE

IF YOU LACK EXPERIENCE, LET ME PAVE THE WAY

LADY EXCUSE ME FOR A MOMENT, MY MIND HAS
FLIPPED

I AM ABOUT TO TAKE YOU INTO SEXUAL BLISS

IT'S LIKE TWISTER, RIGHT HAND BREAST, QUICK
TONGUE PUSSY

AND I WILL NOT STOP UNTIL I FEEL I'M READY

YOU HAVE ME SO EXCITED BY THE PERFUME
YOU WEAR

SO I'LL MAKE YOU SCREAM WITHOUT PULLING
YOUR HAIR

WHILE WE MAKE THE ROOM SPIN, WITH EVERY STROKE

THERE IS NOTHING BUT SWEAT, POURING OFF US BOTH

I THEN SLOW DOWN THE PACE, SO I CAN MASSAGE HER LIPS

THEN HIT ALL HER SPOTS UNTIL SHE CAN'T TAKE IT

ALL THE IMPORTANT HOLES ARE, BEING FITTED FOR SIZE

SHE WANTED A BEAUTIFUL NIGHT, AND I WAS GLAD TO ABLIGE

THERE WERE NO INTERRUPTIONS, DURING WHAT WAS INSTORE

IN THE DOGGYSTYLE POSITION, ALL OF THE SHEETS, SHE TORE

SHE HAD THREE ORGASMS; NOW HERE COMES HER LAST

THE FREAK IN HER, JUST SCREAMED OUT, SPANK MY ASS

HER LEGS ARE STILL SHAKING, AND WE'RE ALMOST DONE

IT WAS COMPLETE XTASCY, THAT MADE ME WANNA CUM

BLAST OFF

"SEX APPEAL"

AS SOON AS SHE STEPPED IN, I CORNERED HER

TO PRONOUCE THAT THIS NIGHT BELONGS
TO ME

AND SHE KNOWS EXACTLY WHAT I AM AFTER

SO, SHE MAKES THAT FACE, THAT IS SO SEXY

THEN, I GENTLY TEASE HER WITH MY TONGUE

IN THOSE TENDER SPOTS THAT GET HER GOING

AND SHE KNOWS EXACTLY WHERE I'M
COMING FROM

NOW WHAT CAN I DO TO GET HER JUICES
FLOWING?

THEN I SPIDER MY WAY DOWN HER TUMMY

IN A STRAIGHT LINE, BUT IN A CIRCLER MOTION

TO REACH THE SWEETNESS THAT IS SO YUMMY

IN TIME, SHE WOULD SEEM AS IF SHE WAS
FLOATING

FROM THE FEELINGS THAT I WOULD CREATE
INSIDE

HER LANGUAGE OF LOVE THAT CAN'T KISS BACK

BUT THEN, SHE POSITIONED HERSELF TO MOUNT
A RIDE

AND WE WENT WAY PASS THE TERM, BEING IN
THE SACK

FOR, EVERYTHING THAT HAPPENED, INCREASED
20 TIMES

JUST FROM THE WAY THAT THIS WOMAN MADE
ME FEEL

CAUSE BOY DID SHE **<u>BLOW</u>** MORE THAN
MY MIND

AND THAT ADDED MORE TO THIS WOMAN'S **<u>SEX
APPEAL</u>**

SMOKING!!!

www.ingramcontent.com/pod-product-compliance
Lightning Source LLC
Chambersburg PA
CBHW021207130726
47988CB00002B/549